Leaves of life
(Poetry)

By:
Tursunali Rahmonov

© Taemeer Publications LLC
Leaves of life
by: Tursunali Rahmonov
Edition: August '2023
Publisher:
Taemeer Publications LLC (Michigan, USA / Hyderabad, India)

ISBN 978-93-5872-136-2

© Taemeer Publications

Book : **Leaves of life** *(Poetry)*
Author : **Tursunali Rahmonov**

Publisher : Taemeer Publications
Year : '2023
Pages : 176
Title Design : *Taemeer Web Design*

Rahmonov Tursunali Otagozievich was born on March 25, 1959 in Khojand district, Torakorgan district, Namangan region, in a peasant family.

In 1977-1982, he graduated from the Faculty of Physics and Technology of Namangan State University. He is a teacher of physics and general technical sciences.

Toragorgan district has started working in 29 schools. Along with educating the young generation, it has been making a worthy contribution to increasing the spiritual and cultural potential of students.

During the years 2012~2020, He received letters of thanks and certificates of honor from regional, district administration and public education department. He worked flawlessly as a school director, deputy in charge of spirituality, creative teacher, and achieved high results in science Olympiads and creative spiritual exams.

A number of poems from his own work are written by him to improve children's spirituality. He regularly participates in regional, national and international competitions.

For example, on January 28, 2022, a collection of poems was published in the Coach's diary, while the poems of his student Khakimboeva Mehrinsa were published in the Children's World diary. At the same time, his students took part in "Smile" children's magazine, "Primary teachers" telegram channel, "The most exemplary artist", "My contribution to the development of the country" competition and were awarded with a thank you letter and a certificate.

Tursunali Rahmonov actively participated in the international competitions of the Republic of Kazakhstan three times "For international services" and He was awarded the "Golden Eagle" and "Friendship of Peoples" badges. As part of the international multidisciplinary scientific and practical conference on "Problems in the era of globalization and their innovative solutions" held in April, he won the international badge "Innovative Promoter", ID digital certificate, certificate, diploma and a collection of articles. He has been participating widely with articles, innovative projects, and poems. New release "Thank you" and other poems are also included in the book.

Alisher Navoi, Babur, Zulfiya, Muhammad Yusuf has been participating in contests announced on the occasion of the birthdays of writers with his poems and articles.

He was filmed on Jizzakh TV as the winner of the contest of republican creators held in Jizzakh. For two years, propagandists on creative and cultural issues have been taking part in the Republican competition.

He won the gratitude award of the spiritual department of Jizzakh region. He was awarded the medal "Sacrifice of his profession" for his worthy participation in the international contest between CIS countries held by the Institute of Scientific Research. At the moment, "Toragorgon student and creative youth" is working on creating a collection of poems and stories and the history of the school where he works, as well as the books "Khojandim dilbandim".

Currently, he is working as a promoter on creative and cultural issues in 43 schools of Torakorgon district.

HAPPY DOUBLE WEDDING MY PRESIDENT.

Peace and prosperity of my country

People's freedom in Uzbek land

The happiness of every household.

My President, congratulations on the double wedding.

After the difficult and difficult years

Remembering great grandfathers.

Independence station, arriving at the destination

President, happy birthday.

It is resistant to any test

The text is strong-willed, with a steady pace.

In terms of politics, he is quick-witted

President, blessed presidency.

For one compact soil of the motherland

For the honor of our country, for the flag.

For the leaf of the thousand-year-old maple

President, happy birthday.

He bet his life on the happiness of his people

He made a bold path to my new Uzbek.

From the present generation, the future awaits

President, blessed presidency.

A common whole with independence

Thirty years have passed, the motherland today

Don't let sadness stay in your heart.

President, happy birthday.

The son of the country from the Uzbeks

A symbol of pride, a symbol of the nation.

Holy dates, all over the country

President, blessed presidency.

God made you Uzbek

He spread your name to the worlds.

He drew attention to the borders

President, happy birthday.

Let him be amazed, the whole world

Hands on our chests, let's send the word.

Greetings from the people of Namangan

My President, congratulations on the double wedding.

The ninth of July, a historic date

The criterion of justice, found the ceremony

Our eyes are burning with great news

My President, congratulations on the double wedding.

July 24 ~ the birthday of the President of the Republic of Uzbekistan Shavkat Miromonovich Mirziyoyev.

Shavkat Miromonovich Mirziyoyev was declared the winner according to the results of the election of the President of the Republic of Uzbekistan on July 9.

TEACHER FROM A REMOTE VILLAGE.

He makes it from a child, as if he were a great potter

In the sky of knowledge, a shining crescent

Good generosity, honest love

Teacher of a remote village.

A great genius in the mind of a child

Don't let it be his heart

Let's appreciate the teacher's work

Teacher of a remote village.

In child talk, you become a child

When he cries you cry, when he laughs you laugh

Tell me you will get this patience

Teacher of a remote village.

Your helpful education is commendable

In intelligence, ingenuity, incomparable, beauty

We know that we don't need too much wealth

Teacher of a remote village.

Better school than home

A classroom, a student, a book

Eh, the nobility of a simple village

Teacher of a remote village.

Take a step into the future now

Education is in thought, step by step

Stay healthy, don't get tired, I'm patient

Teacher of a remote village.

Let's help the teacher

Have we ever asked, his livelihood is low

The teacher's eyes are not moist

Teacher of a remote village.

I'M CLIMBING ROCKS.

I climb over rocks.

I'm going in a hurry with the winds

I overflow like Oman

I'm trying, I'm trying.

I climb over rocks

The eagle is an example, the king of the sky

I have my prey in my stomach

My condolences to Andalab.

I climb over rocks

Not pisand spikes.

So you can't come, cry, ukis

The helpless, they do.

I break through rocks

I'll swim across

I cross the clouds

I will surpass your imagination.

LAST DAY OF SPRING.

The spring whispers slowly at night

He asked permission to leave.

Now you have come, one step at a time

Don't say goodbye, stay for a while.

O bride of the seasons

It's good for you that you taught me.

O ifor, flower pox

How can you stand what you said.

If you are tired, I will ask "summer".

Stay with me for three more months.

Whatever you say, look at it that way

Take my feelings, my pain.

My heart shines in your presence

The surroundings are beautiful and green.

If you leave, the country will miss you

A yellow carpet in the fields.

I can't find it, it's spring

May you stay in Lolazor, Jamal.

Anyway, I can't wait

Abandon it, wipe the horn.

THE WORLD IS BEAUTIFUL, PLAY CHILD.

(June 1 is International Children's Day.)

Children are a handful

Let him play, it's a toy.

Kakajanim, bracelet in hand

A lot of dolls in the nursery.

The world is beautiful, let the child play

Can't get enough of toys, boy.

Kazakh, Uzbek, Latvian, Japanese.

Russian

Armenian, German, Turkmen, Belarusian

Portuguese, Chinese, French too

English, Abyssinian, and Kyrgyz.

Let the multinational world play

Don't miss the toy.

War should not be lit

Peace, friendship, and joy are needed.

The world needs more children

We need flowers, we need a lawn.

May the world rest in peace, child

Can't get enough of toys, boy.

Share love with children

Pretend to grow up.

Play as a crawling horse

Children, speak in groups.

Give the world to the children

A bright future.

KOSHQANOT.

My two great zabardast people

He has "Koshkanoti" in his arms.

With my hand on my chest, I say my song

Best wishes for the future.

Uzbek~Kazakh, the president is today

John is kindred, supreme virtue.

The heart is close, don't be a knot

Kazakh-Uzbek friendship is an example.

.

The sun is shining on your face

The whole world loves you.

Applause to you, glory to you

"Koshkhanotim" is a real ziya.

Long years, bright world

Double your wings and fly away.

Creativity is embodied in it

Embrace beauty and happiness.

ANTHEM OF KOSHQANOT CREATIVE FOUNDATION.

My two great people, great faith

Your roots are strong, you are a great maple.

Let the ancestors use it, eternal happiness and luck

Dear Koshkhanot, you are the pride of the nation.

Life is a bond of kinship, a supreme virtue

Uzbek-Kazakh friendship, wisdom is also an example

Pearls and emeralds offered by two peoples

Dear Koshkhanot, you are a visionary of the people.

Today the whole world loves you

My double-winged mother, a true soul

Applause, congratulations, my eyes are bright

Dear Koshkhanot, the people are waiting for you.

Long years, of course, this world is bright

Creativity, people of inspiration, gathered together

Talent, talent is embodied.

Dear Koshkhanot, giant of the people.

TELL THE ADVERTISEMENT WHAT TO DO NOW

It's not a sight, tell me what's going on

He was shocked to read, he is poor

His head is spinning, his imagination is restless

Tell me, what should the propagandist do now?

You have been writing and spreading the word

You were creating new names

You were focusing on your creativity and inspiration

Tell me, what should the propagandist do now? .

He was restless, the example was lively

This wrist is strong and tireless

Work and enthusiasm should be appreciated.

Tell me, what should the propagandist do now?

What is the sin of the propagandist people

Is he an unnecessary stone, who is his refuge?

Ten thousand propagandists, who is the question?

Tell me, what should the propagandist do now?

Today the propagandist mourns at home

The tea he drank was bitter and tasteless

Help us, Gulnoza

Tell me, propagandist, what should he do now? .

He rushed to the street, promoting poor

He has a salty forehead

If possible, do something.

Tell the propagandist, what should he do now?

SYMPATHY

Natural phenomenon, forest fire

It caught fire, from a lightning strike.

My Kazakh brother, Abai Akin

The cry is in my ear, from fourteen graves.

Peace, you have stepped into the green

Mardu~ your field will not go away for nothing.

Always proud of the country

Uzbek brother is sympathetic, you are not alone.

A little girl was left an orphan, a Kazakh child

Desperate bride's cry.

Father and mother moan in silence

Recite to the souls of the departed.

Since it is a day of mourning, let us sympathize

Unlimited respect to our Kazakh master.

Let's be a neighbor, like-minded, helper

Mourning my neighbor, mourning for us too.

(I express my deepest condolences to the people of Kazakhstan. Lives in Khojand Mfy, Torakorgan District)

POETRY OF APPEAL.

A name from history, the profession of propaganda

You won't find it in the Red Book either.

It's okay, it's a sweet memory

As it is the work of fate, we will not be disappointed

A plan for the new school year

Photos for each event.

Talented boy, sure result

We used to go to meetings together.

Contribution to the development of the country

We tied our waists to spiritual work

My soul is devoted to a perfect generation

Help yourself, let's go.

Someone writes poetry, someone sings

He reads the text well and is surprised.

Even with a small salary, we are all happy

The dream is a mirage, and our hearts are broken.

The salty baby is not even three years old

Tomorrow is our day, winter, prison.

Our heart is pure, transparent, a spring

Things were going well, we were happy.

Hey uncles sitting on top

Please return the state.

Well, you don't need a lot of money

Please listen, come to help.

Address poem of republican propagandists on creative and cultural issues.

OTPUSNOY FALLS.

The sun shone in his sad eyes

Loakal had an opportunity, he was excited

It's not too late, hope

Hurray propagandist, retired.

What to do, it's going to be sad

He doesn't like it, he doesn't go to the wedding

Finding a new job will be a race

The poor man got a little otpusnoy.

He doesn't care about vacation pay

A friend from another position is disappointed

He beckons with his hand, says the word arrow

Okay, even if it's a little, it's a farewell.

Talent disappeared, poetry died

We have reached the address, the place is full

Working time is over, let's go

If Ordona stays, he will leave.

Mardikor market is waiting for us

"Do you have any work?" Zir runs

Russia is waiting, immigrant, now

He left without reaching the road.

MY FATHER IS PRAISED.

I opened my eyes, I saw, it's amazing

My father is worthy of praise.

My father, my soul

I feel your love every moment.

You caress, you never melt

You have time for me early or late.

Life is fun, this world is beautiful

My father is better than everyone else.

I was born, my father is one side

My father is crying a lot around me.

If I'm angry, if I'm angry

He does not fight, he endures every moment.

I'm still young, a kindergarten child

Those who gave birth, a grain of sugar.

Father~ mother, grandmothers every time

They say, a wrestler is a lamb.

A big guy, of course

My dreams are as big as the sky.

I will serve and receive blessings

I will be a wing to my father.

Heart to grandson Abrorbek, beloved father Bahromjon

statements.

He lives in the village of Khojand in the Torakorgan district

ASLIJODKOR.

In the range of Great Turkestan

In the earthquake of Shahri Sayrami

In the book of Ahmad Yassavi.

A person is born, a valley of happiness

Know that in the future, the genius of nations.

He is the son of the nation, who is honored by the nation

He is the page of history, the son of nations

He is the son of the people whose world is shining

Rebel against creation, ask the Eldor

Inspiration fairies are coming, look.

Kingdom of creation, star of light

Nazm is also a torch in navo

Every word is as sharp as Babur's sword.

Your birthday is summer

A true creator is born in the summer.

Director of the "Koshkhanot" fund of creators of Kazakhstan, Uzbekistan.

Worker of culture who served in Kazakhstan

I sincerely congratulate Tatiev Eldorbek on his birthday on June 20.

I welcome the great goal of uniting the artists of the two nations. I wish you good health and success in your good work.

OTANOLASI.

You haven't seen your father, my daughter, little girl

White as the moon, pure in heart, innocent white spring.

You don't really know me, I left when you were one year old

I violated the great and pure name of father.

If you can forgive your father, forgive me, angel

Heart and soul are close,

an inseparable bond.

Stupid father, I am unloving, I did not protect my family

I did not take the advice of my parents and relatives.

They blinded my eyes, you unfaithful fellows

I'm in a hurry, without an appointment, and I'm in trouble.

My days have become drunken when the tannoz woman is in pain

I wish you a good night, my dear mother.

Wealth made me stutter, I couldn't stop.

I didn't pay attention to this faithful mother of yours.

The deed is gone, the reputation is gone, it's all a mirage.

A cunning woman drove away, everything was ruined.

When I say walk, walk my way,

I don't have a home.

I don't have enough money to make a living.

Your mother has not forgiven me, I know she will not forgive me.

I will present a loaqal ring to my daughter.

Murgak is dedicated to fathers who have left their children, and life as a flower has left their wives.

You are the pride of Uzbekistan, my dear child.

This land is so beautiful, the sky is so bright

Love is one side, generosity is one side.

You are a product of my upbringing, the country needs you every moment.

You are the pride of Uzbekistan, my soul child.

Multinational, children of Uzbekistan are united

You work in the heat of the hot palm, you are healthy.

You are creative, creative, great result, quantity~ quality.

You are the pride of Uzbekistan, my dear child.

I am a mother, may my children grow up in the homeland

Have a healthy future, I'll see you soon.

I am a mother, a servant who prays for refuge.

You are the pride of Uzbekistan, my dear child.

May no dust settle on your honorable Uzbek name

Let there be no sorrow in a peaceful house.

Don't give in to indifference.

You are the pride of Uzbekistan, my dear child.

LET'S UNITE.

June 30 ~ YOUTH DAY.

Come on friends, let's go hand in hand

Progress, to the bright path to the goal.

Let's strive for a happy palace of life

Let's ask the creator for strength.

We are young people, our compatriots are our trust

Mother earth, our support for tomorrow.

This koshana inherited from ancestors

Let's be brave, burn with enthusiasm.

We are young people, the fortress of the motherland is an idol

My mother nation, expect results from your generation.

Our goal, good will, strong knowledge

Honest work, ingenuity is a test of science.

A new vision in the youth of the new age

Every age has the right to be happy and proud.

Let's unite friends towards a higher goal

Let's sing a happy land.

HELLO, HERBIM.

(July 2~the day of adoption of the State Coat of Arms of the Republic of Uzbekistan).

You are the symbol of Uzbekistan, my coat of arms

I'm free, a peaceful life, speak for yourself, my dear

I wish you a bright future, my dear

The pride of my country, salute my coat of arms.

You have a Humo bird that is looking for the blue

The song of the hymn, the dutor sings

The nation lives in peace and is clean

The pride of my country, salute my coat of arms.

Uzbekistan, what a loving heart

This is a heavenly country, my people need it

Awesome 31 year old, great wrist

The pride of my country, salute my coat of arms.

On one side is a cotton field, on the other side is a grain field

There is a dear sun with open arms for blessing

Love in the heart, pure heart, conscience, honor

The pride of my country, salute my coat of arms.

Deep blue nature, clear sky

Amu birla Sir, the source of which is medicine

Faith in religion

The pride of my country, salute my coat of arms.

The flag of the country in strong hands

Covered with flowers, every fat of the country

Supporter, trust, dear head of state

The pride of my country, salute my coat of arms.

TWO SWALLOWS.

Two swallows near the sun

I woke up from a deep roar.

He said, sustenance has arrived, open your gate

I thanked the morning messenger.

Singer of freedom, angel of freedom

The wheel is flying, your wings are flapping.

In your tiny heart, a precious bond

From the visit to the apartment, please.

A pair of swallows on the roof of the yard

A little polapon under the wing.

A long willow tree was a guest for him

Dear birds, the home has become the homeland.

It happens that every season is spring

Come to Karakashim, I'll wait for you, Mushtaq.

Happiness is the ambassador of spring, let's repeat

I miss you and the porch.

You came from afar without getting tired

Iran, or China, maybe India.

A quiet place in peace, you chose, you know

Ocean of peace, peaceful Uzbekistan.

A SOLDIER'S FATHER.

(Watching the Georgian film "Soldier's Father" named after the Second World War).

Soldier father looking for his son

Chance got lost, on the way to the front.

A pipe with a fist, a tobacco pouch

The knot named for his son is in his hand.

Wounded. Hospital. Hero boy

Maharashvili, Georgian descent.

Tank division, guard of the country

The father's son is also a native of Goderdze.

Soldat's father is kind and brave

He was not afraid of the fate of his son.

Gun in hand, goes proudly

From the fire from enemy weapons.

The last episode, the four-story house

All three floors, surrounded by Germans.

At that moment, a Georgian tune was played

The regiment was ready to attack, but it stopped.

The father called out, "Who's up there?"

The soldiers rushed to attack the enemy.

"Surrounded by the father" there are friends and me

Ahiri found his son who played the tune.

The father rushed to attack like a tiger

The building was cleared. the enemy was killed

The lifeless body of the son, pressed into his arms.

Father and son were given badges.

WE ARE GOING TO SEE MY FATHER.

It's a sister, get it together

I'm leaving, take a look.

Are you ready, my sister, let's go

We will go to see my father

What's up, let's go and ask.

Three girls, who has my father

Do not treat anyone as a child

Look at the snow-white heads

We are going to see my mother

Father is at home, we will stay until today.

A suit~ pants suit for my father

Shut up, don't tell me about your shoes

"We're here" mom who's home

We are going to see my father.

We will keep you updated.

We are all princesses in every house

Bride of the wide house, angel

My family is very happy

We are going to see my mother.

We'll have a chat.

Happy birthday, my dear

Laugh with joy together

Let's not be a girl, son

We are going to see my father

We will take care of your pain.

Daughters wrote in Shahnoza language as a birthday greeting to their father Ma'murjon.

KAMOLJON TURGUNOV.

Such an apartment in my neighboring village

Is this man a legend, a war hero?

I still have terrible memories

Uzbek hero Father Kamoljon.

The house is like a museum, pictures, objects

Words from the horror of war story

What I said is not true

War hero, father Kamoljon.

Stalingrad. Sapcha head snake charm

Towards Pavlov's house, enemy attack

Supposedly, all the Russians were killed

An ordinary Uzbek soldier, Father Kamoljon.

A Russian woman who eats bullets is a lifeless joker

A baby soul in the bosom of the vines

No one can help now

Uzbek hero, Father Kamoljon.

Uzbek haloskor, Father Kamoljon

Battle-hardened, fierce fire

He couldn't wait patiently

Heartbreaking, father Kamoljon.

He ran and grabbed the girl by the waist

Boiling blood spewed from the soldier's hand

Death also retreated from the path of the brave

A true hero, Father Kamaljon.

In front of Lieutenant Pavlov's house

That infamous memory is in his mind

Anna gave birth to a child

Hero Pavlov chi Kamoljon father.

Anna, the face of Kamaljon's father

He comes to visit himself

Although she is Russian, she is the daughter of Bordimkol

Battle of Stalingrad, Father Kamoljon.

This poetic dedication is dedicated to the memory of Kamoljon Turgunov from Bordimkol, a hero of the Second World War, a participant in the defense of the legendary Pavlov House.

Toychi Eryigitov.

(The hero soldier Toychi Eryigitov, a participant in the war, died heroically by blocking a German machine gun with his gun.)

German Fortification, Dzot, Machine Gun.

Incessant bullet rain, the sound is incessant.

Do not raise your head, lie firmly on the ground

The surroundings are flat like a meadow, and there is no grass.

Machine gun fire cannot be extinguished

Someone died, someone died.

It's been three hours, it's late in the evening

Shivering, immediately, blood on the chest.

Bloody fire from Dzot

Destroy two thousand soldiers.

Death stopped his voice, someone

Who is the guard who stopped the fascist?

The commander shouted, go forward

Run over the enemy, open fire.

Anger is an arrow of anger, run away if you are angry

It is true that the voice of death has stopped

Blessed blood covering the chest.

This guy is holding his chest to the enemy

May the hero of the nation be honored

Uzbek hero Toychi Eryigit.

OFARIN.

(Two artists from Namangan 11th school in Uychi district, publicist Alisher Joraev and publicist Muyassar Ergasheva of the 67th school in Chust district won the highest place in the republican stage of the contest "The Most Valuable Publicist".)

The people of Targibatchi, the honor of Namangan

Poor, hardworking, intelligent, smart

To the front lines, forward everyone

Well done, Alisher brother.

Intelligent, leader, creator

Today, the Creator has become a helper

There is a right to victory, victory, good luck

Well done Alisher, my sister Muyassar.

They are the real devil of poetry

The meaning of chors for lively conversation

We are all in awe, the highest grade

Well done, Alisher brother.

Handsome, educated, handsome

We definitely admire them

The idea of spirituality, a deep principle

Well done Alisher, my sister Muyassar.

Go to school, poet

One plays a tune, the other a circle

Singer Shahjahan, artist Naila

Well done, Alisher brother.

He is not a winner for nothing, the experience is great

First time on the promotional scene

We are happy with them

Well done Alisher, my sister Muyassar.

Melodies, a festival of flowers

Flower to flower double, spring time

The people of Namangan rejoice

Well done, Alisher brother.

NAMANGANDA FLOWER FESTIVAL.

(The Namangan International Flower Festival will begin on May 21.)

Ato is a guest, great as a father

Welcome to visit

One land, one goal

Namanganda flower festival.

Guests from all over the world

Applause, flower garden Ajam

No doubt, heaven Eram

Namanganda flower festival.

Red, yellow, white, various

Lily of the valley, basil, carnation

Father ~ mother, my children go.

Namanganda flower festival

Khainchalak, sky dome

Niagara Falls, Gulf of the Nile

The color miracle of the seven rainbows

Yuryng Namangan Flower Festival.

Namangan pilaf, see here

In Parvar, suck holwa, novvot

Come with me if you don't believe me

Let's celebrate the flower festival in Namangan.

Babur Park, a legend

You are drunk with flowers, mastona

Your eyes are burning with color

Let's celebrate the flower festival in Namangan.

All kinds of flowers are here

Namanganim gulsevar elda

I will give you a flower of heaven, come

Walk, Namangan Flower Festival.

Charming flower, beautiful flowers

Sister, children are happy

The singers sing songs

Namanganda flower festival.

This happens every season

My flowers have a reflection of the sun

UZBEKISTAN, green spring

Namanganda flower festival.

LAST CALL.

May 25, last call

Greetings, my dear teachers

I bow to you, but in my heart

Last call, it hurts.

May 25, last call

My friend of 11 years, goodbye comrade.

My heart is beating, my heart is white

Goodbye, my love, you were my confidant.

May 25, the last call

I start moving towards the dream ~ goal.

I have a pass in my hand, a great passion

I read, with joy, tears in my eyes.

May 25, last call

My intelligence, my glory is my school.

The sky of dreams, the future is bright

My school is full of love.

May 25, the last call

Last call, play the tune.

The ringing of the bell, our intention is pure

Receive blessings from the teacher.

FARRUKH

I know a guy

Do whatever you can.

Cute, alpine, carefree

Dear friends, it's hard for him.

Organizer at school

Event ~ head to the meeting.

The captain of the neighborhood

He doesn't have a heart.

He makes something out of nothing

He persuades the unaccustomed.

The eyes are smiling

Makes sweet conversation.

A prayer from the father every day

Mehrigiya from mother.

A strong young family

Small home circle.

Husband and wife are double wings

The girl is a sweet girl.

The offspring of the victim's father.

Underneath is a horse.

This young man is ambitious

We expect hope from him.

Farrukh, good luck

May you have a future.

IT'S SUMMER SEASON.

(To the selection).

This world is actually four wonders

Each season will be manifested in the season.

Summer has started here in our country

The temperature of the sun spread everywhere.

Jonahon summer is the month of blessings

Various fruits reddened by the heat.

Cool resorts, holiday month

Fountains in the evening, gentle lovers.

Head from the harvest, a field with wheat

Come to the Labor Front, please.

From the grain caravan, the warehouses are full

Good luck to the untiring Uzbek.

My land is an open table in the world

A hard-working farmer, his work is in vain.

His house is full, when a guest comes

The kind summer season leaves a trail.

Uzbek summer for three whole months

Winter thoughts for tomorrow.

He gathers his harvest and does not stand alone

Uzbek weddings are also suitable.

IF I GO TO SAMARKAND.

Every time I go to Samarkand

Ash'or is finished, I have a notebook in my hand.

I will see Ulugbek again

I will say a word of prayer.

And at the gate of Samarkand

Opposite Ulugbek.

I saw the spirit of Islam

I was talking to my father.

One is a horn, another is a horn

Both are great kings.

He sacrificed his life for the country

He took an oath for the happiness of the people.

Both geniuses from Samarkand

Indescribable, perfect tancho.

Worship, two great ones

Make your soul happy for a lifetime.

Leaves of life, your name is golden

A universal statue was placed.

Uzbekistan is an inheritance from you

Gulshan aro achilar qigos.

IYMON.

Bismillah Rahmanu Rohiym

Sincerely, my sincere greetings.

Awwzu billah shaitan rojiim

Kalimai shahadat kalam.

We have no body, our soul is eternal

Our way goes to eternity.

A dead body in a coffin

We are generous, our hands are open.

It rained, it rained all day and night

Bandalik, a Muslim woman.

The loved ones are close to the heart

"Am I now" you think is an illusion.

Pray, pray

Here is the key to heaven.

Know that this world is transitory

Teaching a believer to a brother.

Hadmi Koran, religious ritual

His servants seek refuge.

A luxurious luxury style

He looks down on the creator.

We are servants, the world is fine

We hear, we do not act.

Fun, fun, fun

We don't know if it's heaven or not.

A person who calls to faith

The prestige and honor of my neighborhood.

The lecture is excellent, my brother Adhamjon

It means that he speaks in the way of truth

RASHTJAN.

February 18, 1957.

February 18, 9023.

(little joke)

Riding a bicycle

Rashitjon went on the road.

Hanging a rose on the steering wheel

Gonadi, Tatarstan.

Driving fast

He turned to Chistopol.

Suddenly he was on his way

He hit Mallasoch.

Hitting is an excuse

He hooked the Russian girl.

He lived a great life, Shoshona

Stayed together for a lifetime.

Happiness is luck in the Tatar land

They lived without medicine.

Health on this day

Rashit is over sixty.

Grandparent ~ grandmother

His children are happy.

Sharing generosity

Currently in service.

Aziz was born on the day

Let's go sweet word.

From all friends, you know

Greetings to Rashitjon.

Our dear fellow student, Akhmetov Rashitni, 66 years old, currently living in the city of Chistopol, Republic of Tatarstan, previously living in the village of Kyzilravot, Uychi District, Namangan Region.

Happy Thanksgiving everyone

friends sincerely congratulate.

B O B U R Sh O X .

B~ Spring is at the flower festival

I would like to finish

O~ Finally walking one by one

I would like to wait for you

B~ Who is the innocent angel,

do not destroy the heart

He gave his life to creation

don't let your heart wander

R~ If your opponent is a hawk, you are an eagle

Sh~ On a horse with a horn, hit and become deaf

O~ It's not easy, Boburnama

Let's define it

X~ At that time when Harna does

let's choose with a pen

BLESSED DAUGHTER.

One in my heart

The rose has opened.

He is the only one in the world

It was scattered.

This is a beautiful rose

Dilbandim da Mubarak.

Light in my neighborhood

Iodine act "Congratulations".

Excellent at Oliygosh

The heart is pure and innocent.

What he said is meaningful

Conscience, honor, modesty, etc.

I am a mother, my daughter

I will be patient

After all, I'm on my face

I see pure love.

My sweet girl, my soul girl

The work he did is good.

Science ocean, mine girl

Girls are angels.

Head of two brothers

Sweet language boy.

Guide in "Ziya Nur".

Every moment teaches.

Oraz, elegant appearance

Pink face, cute.

Sirat is a strange expression

His students are sweet.

Our family is one world

Sample, ahil~inoq.

I am princess, your father is Khan

Our day is happy and cheerful.

You are my future, my pride

My glasses, Mubarak.

My covenant, my throne, my happiness

Happy birthday.

Marguba G'furova congratulates Jigarbandi Mubarak, who was born on February 16.

My pride is Shahandi.

Ask us for sugar and honey

Wrap pashmak holvo on open tables

The market is full of sweets, sweets

see the language

I am the confectioner you know from Shahand.

Good intentions, dreams and desires are characteristic of a real person

Look, I made a crib, suitable for a small child

I'm still young, I'm a craftsman, I still have little skills

I am the same craftsman you know from Shahand.

Take the oven full of sour bread

Stay in Shahandim, knowing its taste and content

Have patir bread, hole cake, for breakfast

I'm Shahandlik, that baker brother you know.

The mother misses the land, the farmer needs a hoe.

A belt on the waist, a shovel,

iron shears to the gardener

A blade of fire, a fire, heat, fire

I am a temir bukkan from Shahand

your brother who lit the fire.

I made a blanket and sewed a palak, a white scarf on my dear head

The bride's dowry, the flower bouquet that she made at the wedding

The lovely girls in Shahand are beautiful, and the moon is beautiful

I am Shahsana, a craftswoman you know from Shahand.

In the embroidered train, the master was waiting for his wife

Eastern woman, hope for the future is over

For the happiness of his family, he won the farewell

I am Gulsana, a young bride you know from Shahand.

Koklam has arrived, a swallow is circling in the sky

Tanovaru, Dilhiroj's dark hair

Sing the song of happiness

I'm Malohat, a hairy girl you know from Shakhand.

First the food, then the cook,

my hands are sweet

Try the chocolate cake, the cake

We have a lot of pastries, let's go and get them

I'm Latofat, a cook you know from Shakhand.

EARTHQUAKE

It shook involuntarily, a strong earthquake

High houses are complete, slaves are in basements

Ruined streets, full of corpses

It happened in Jabrdi, my neighbor is Turkish.

Maybe there are many sinners, maybe you are innocent

Thousands of households, no longer safe

A prayer to the Lord, the hands are countless

Dear Turkish people, who was in Jabrdi.

Our life is a test, a time scale

We are a sinful servant, what can we say

My brother's heart is stained today

My friend, who was in Jabrdi, is Turkish.

Before God, I am a weak servant

Let's not do it in vain

Patience, thanks, we are alive today

My neighbor in Jabrdi is a Turk.

This is God's will

Tell the Turks, that's it

so

Turks wear shirts, Uzbeks wear collars

Dear Turkish people who were in Jabrdi.

Friend to brother, kindness

It is an oriental custom to lend a helping hand

Consequence, generosity, necessity, respect

My friend who was in Jabrdi is a Turk.

It was written to express sympathy to the Turkish people, who were devastated by a strong earthquake on February 6.

Koshkairagoch village.

I remember my thoughts

I remember the history of my village

I will stay in the village forever

Koshkayraghoch is my native village,

My dear, honorable father.

It has been called Koshkairagoch since ancient times

Mamadali mentions my grandfather

I feel that he is a selfless person

Koshkairagokh is my native village.

There are hardworking people with a wide heart

There are apples and almonds in the garden

He has a hand on his chest and words on his tongue

My dear, honorable father.

Don't plow, generous peasants

Do not be weary in doing good

Never miss the sustenance that Allah has given you

Koshkairagoch, my native village.

There are brides with beautiful words and expressions
He gets up early, milks the cow, bakes bread
Sacrifice your life for your bride, that's what brides do
My dear, honorable father.

Children go to kindergarten
Sweets will live and grow happily
The rich of the village buy tall houses
Koshkairagoch is my native village.

He teaches the young generation, his teachers
Navo words are played and sung
Have a happy autumn, winter, spring and summer
My dear, honorable father.

Scholars and leaders came from here
Entrepreneurship has always been inherited from the father
It was thought that he should be knowledgeable

Koshkairagoch is my native village.

The girls of our village do not get tired of working

Hush polite, yellow flower-like faces

His emerald eyes are ashamed of love

My dear, honorable father.

My grandfather planted a sycamore tree that reached the sky

Glorifying the people of "GOSH".

he looked at the maple tree

He created goodness under the name of Koshkairagoch

Koshkairagoch is my native village

My dear, honorable father.

GULIMONOLOGI.

"Obeisance to Hazrat Navoi"

to the selection.

I am a Turk, an Uzbek girl

I am proud of my parents

Alisherni's words.

Yes, I am that, that Guli.

Long nights, candlelight

O'shal Begum, Sanam jilvasi

Khan is from the palace, the hut is preferred

I am that, yes I am a hut.

I put two braids on my hair

Yor burned in the fire

Remained faithful in loyalty

I am faithful, yes I am faithful.

Alisher, my heart is in my bosom

On my right, on my walking path

My heart is in my heart

I am "heart" faith, that Guli.

Sher kelbatli, pahlavan Farhad

Mother's soul is happy and prosperous

Homeland, free and free

I'm Shirin, yes I am.

Ghazal finished, sharp pen

In agony, the pain of parting

Thoughtful, imaginary world

I am pain, I am a writing pen.

Majnun, driven to the desert

Heart for Yori

I was a Laila yesterday

Yes, I am that, that Layli.

I feed from Mozi, that's the time

Jarangi voice, epic of hearts

It won't stop there, my heart is full of peace

I am that Guli, that Guli.

HAPPY BIRTHDAY.

When the sun is shining

When the flower opens and blooms

A smile on your face, a laugh

The sun greets you. Happy birthday

Good intention, perfect child

Reconciliation, flower scarf

May my country be beautiful

Your child sends greetings.

Happy Thanksgiving.

Hard-working, demanding leader at work

There is a real human quality

There is no conscience in our hearts

Greetings on my behalf

Happy birthday.

You are beautiful, queen of flowers

Every word has a deep meaning

A devoted mother to her children

Flowers greet you

May this happy day be blessed.

A wife for your lover

A bird of paradise, like an angel

Love is an unbreakable bond

Greetings from your owner.

Have a blessed day.

You don't have a boss, you're a woman at home

Your tongues are like honey

Your work is recognized

Greetings from the team

May your day be blessed.

Loyalty and loyalty are common

You will be alert to our work

Our kindergarten always needs you

Children say hello

May the birth be blessed.

This dedication is the head of the 24th kindergarten, Polvonova Yakutkhan, was written as a birthday greeting from his beloved student Gulira'na.

SABR.

Patience is the key to heaven

There is such an expression.

The seed of the wise

The happiness of patience is luck.

If you are patient, your wife

Ayhonnosi stops.

If you miss the point, your wife

Deaf is like dumb.

Wait a minute

Even if you break the rules.

Don't rush, go now

Even if your car is great.

When the leader gives a speech

Maybe you are right.

When anger rides a horse

Happy is the patient.

Circle of teachers

Listen politely.

What is velvet?

Pur to understand the meaning.

Every word that has moved from the language

Understand who you are.

Just a word of caution

Someone's tail.

There is a lot to say about patience, you know

Silence is merciful.

Quit being greedy

The language is flawlessly clear.

Application for dismissal

Just think about it.

Innocent, he thought

Listen to your heart.

Your anger is right under your nose

Stop, shut up right now.

You can explode

You need health, know that.

Do not fall in love with the house net

There are those who are greater than you.

Don't be too wordy

Every word has weight

Do not hang on a high gallows

Asta pillapoya.

Be careful, don't rush

From the stairwell.

Be patient

Signs of life content.

Strong, patient

Lines in the heart.

LIKE A GHAZAL.

"Obeisance to Hazrat Navoi" Koshkhanot international competition.

N A V O I Y.

N~Navoi Guli was killed at the head of a spring

A~Ahdu~payman brought the jug to the spring.

V~ If there is a loyal person, everyone is in love

O~The taffeta of the sun is together, in the string of the heart.

I~Praising two hearts is the work of good people

Y~The road is far, the life is long, the heart is over.

G U L I.

G~Gulgun is happy to see you

May your life flourish.

A pinch of laughter on L~La'li's lips

I~ Love is a stirring feeling.

YOUNG ENTREPRENEUR.

Entrepreneurship comes from the father

The right word, honesty, hard work

The merchant is busy, hanging on the shoulder

Brother Bahadir, a businessman from Khojand.

New Uzbekistan is new rich

You are generous, enterprising

Padar~ you love your parents

Khojandlik Khotamtoy, Bahadir brother.

You are the happy throne that God looks at

You are driven towards a clear goal

Love in your heart, you are committed to your duty

Brother Bahadir, who glorified Khojand.

The sun is shining, the sky is kum~kuk

Let it grow, let it bloom, everywhere in the country

Beautiful nature, garden

Brother Bahadir, who improved the country.

He built a hospital to serve

Dardmandu to honor the patient

To be an example to the working people

Praise be to you Bahadir brother.

May your parents always be healthy

Let their tongues be in the word, in prayer

May your heart be full of joy

In El's eyes, Bahadir is a brother.

Don't shy away from kindness to the poor

Don't invest in a waterfall plan

Do not reveal your secret to an untested friend

Dear brother Bahadir.

The trust of the head of state, the trust of the people

Your neighborhood, your blood, your friend's support

The joy of tomorrow's youth

Brother Bahadir, who believes in the future.

This poem was written to praise Bahadir Alisherov, a businessman from Khojand.

SHERDOR PHYSICIANS.

Modern luxury, crystal luxury

Orderly, personable, smart office

The lamb rejoices, the blessed threshold

Well done Sherdar, doctors.

I'm visiting because I'm sick

to the ENT

Accurate diagnosis and treatment are here

There is no question, Akmaljon's knowledge is excellent

Well done Sherdar, doctors.

There is a pharmacy and a side kitchen

Nicely located room and suite

Everything is calculated, everything is transparent

Well done Sherdar, doctors.

A smile on his face, modesty in his eyes

As if the angel of salvation is standing

If you ask her name, her name is Mahliyo

Well done Sherdar, doctors.

The Hippocratic Oath, along with the Koran

Golden sentences, remember every moment

Help the sick, broken hearted

Well done Sherdar, doctors.

There are thousands of patients in the reception

Salvation is an eyesore, a heart is half-hearted

Don't throw a spear at the heart, the hearts are nimta

Well done Sherdar, doctors.

Don't be greedy, honor your conscience, etc

You have the title of doctor

Someone, who is difficult for your great rank

Well done Sherdar, doctors.

Doctoral status is characteristic of your work

God looked, you are reconciled

Always listen to the prayer of the father

Well done Sherdar, doctors.

This poem was written as a tribute to the doctors, nurses and technical staff of the Sherdar hospital of Mingbuloq district.

OPENED IN THE CEMETERY, LOLAQIZGALDO.

A flower opened in the cemetery

Alvon made of human blood

Graves roll, stain on my heart

The moment I saw my mother's grave.

A flower opened in the cemetery

Your wrapped hands, painted tulip.

Golden morning dew, rising sun

A ruby cup that your lips have kissed.

A flower opened in the cemetery

In the gentle shabbos that swayed my hair.

I compare my mother's grave to a garden

And on the windy Shabbat, you are in the temple.

A flower opened in the cemetery

Here I am again at the head of the grave.

As soon as I see it, my heart is happy.

Dear mother, please be patient.

A flower opened in the cemetery

My heart breaks, I have tears in my eyes.

I have a souvenir in my hand, the crutch you gave me.

Let your grave light up, this is the sun forever.

SNIPER GIRL.

I dedicate to the memory of Zebo Ganieva, the hero of the Second World War, the girl Uzbek sniper.

The cold of the night, the stage of winter

A lost owl, a screeching hoot

It is constantly raining, it is snowing

Just a sniper girl, a restless vigilante.

It's been a week, the girl has no sleep

Stvolley gun, girl ain't got no fear

There is no good feeling against the enemy

Just a sniper girl, a restless vigilante.

He is a German general

The fortress is in hand, the plan is realistic

Enemy forehead, take clear aim

Just a sniper girl, restlessly alert.

Finally out of the woods, a light car

A tire burst from the shot

Task completed, last day~ a

Just a sniper girl, a restless vigilante.

A German officer was captured

That's how the fascist plan was revealed

The counterattack plan failed

done

Just a sniper girl, a restless vigilante.

BREST FORT.

41 years. War. Brest Castle

The hole is here, the soldier moaned

A human child who has not seen destruction

The hero city is Brest Castle.

The sky is a dark cloud, arrows viz~vizi

Sprout root

The battle does not stop, yesterday afternoon

The hero city is Brest Castle.

It's blue, it's a bug, it's a handgun

It doesn't come out of his mouth, German cha xal't~xal't

Kombat shouts "Ataka" to the enemy

Hero's Castle, Brest Castle.

There is not water in the river, but blood clots

Burma~ one killed, is there a living soul

Battles for every inch of land are inevitable

The hero fortress is the Brest fortress.

Dropped by a plane, a bomb

Heroes are the soul of young men

Black tanks are creeping up

Hero's Castle, Brest Castle.

Four gates of Brest fortress

Five years of constant gunfire

The enemy did not win, lol

The hero fortress is the Brest fortress.

Heroes of Brest Castle

Generations will not forget those moments

The blood of salvation was not shed in vain

Hero's Castle, Brest Castle.

Go to Brest, my friend

From soldier's blood, crimson tulip

The husband is dead from old age, he laments

Brest Castle is Brest Castle.

THE SOLDIER IN THE TRENCHES.

He was wounded four times, he was not afraid of evil

Ur~yiqit, from the fire coming out of the barrel.

Today will be a very intense battle

Fighting with a tank, the enemy is powerful.

It's early morning, six o'clock

Surprisingly, the enemy also calmed down a bit.

It is raining, it is very wet

The corpses are lying like a lake of blood.

He took a picture from his pocket

The figure of the mother looks surprised.

His hair is gray, his hands are folded

He is picking cotton, he is crying.

He doesn't remember his father, he's just a baby

Mother raised, every day a pillar.

He entered the war before he was eighteen

He knew the horror of death in battles.

Mother bitten in the yard

He took a flower handkerchief from the girl next door.

He wrote a greeting letter on a piece of paper covered with mud

"MOM" I am alive, he wrote a bloody letter.

A fragment of a shell suddenly squealed

Above the trench, a voice roared.

The soldier was mocked, the tank crashed

A letter in his hand, an eternal dream.

This poem was written based on the war memories of my father Otavali Rahmonov, a participant in World War II.

HOLJANDI, HOLIDAY, BLESSED.

(Khojand neighborhood won the initiative open budget project.)

O prosperity of the people of Khojand

The beauty of strong hearts

Strong family happy survival

My dear fellow villager, this is a blessed day

This is the seventh day of Faizli May.

Initiative open, budget started

Either way, he was disappointed

My people were thrown towards the dream goal

Happy holiday my dear fellow villager.

The eyes of the neighborhood, a beautiful child

He is devoted to his father and mother

He showed courage and courage

Happy work, happy holiday.

Bahadir is a real good-natured boy.

Incarnate, like a wrestler

Ready for every task right now.

Dear brother, happy holiday.

Greetings from the Sherdor complex

We send a word to the people of Mingbulok

Hello everyone

Dear Mingbuloq, my dear colleague.

Supermarket, Sardoba, main center

Take it to the right places, guys

Selling girls and Javlonbek

Happy holiday to the supermarkets.

My butcher brothers Bahramboy and Adil

Islam and Abdurasul agreed

Dear people, know what you have done

Happy holiday to a selfless person

Like-minded guys, one flesh and one soul

In short, a brave hero

Effective wandering in 10 days of trial

Happy holiday guys.

My devotion to Daniel and Ilyasbek has increased

I am interested in Dostonbek and Sherzod

Daniyor, I looked at Mamurjon

Khojand pioneers, happy holiday.

Khojand young men are my field

On the stage of the world, my world

If Khojand is a caravan, you are my captain

Khojand activists, happy holiday.

Nurmat, my dear brother

Savob drew a mark in the book

You are the one who holds the reins of merit

Happy holiday to charity.

Alimardan chief, eight points

Unforgettable moments of sound

Young people, heroes of our time

Happy holiday to the students.

The lake is in our chest, the school is for the team

Muzaffar, Azamat, to the leader

Dear coaches, everyone

Thank you, my dear school.

Our greatest strength, mother

Your hard work is not wasted

My nursery, a solid rock

We bow to you Sevara Oya.

There is a movement to gather votes

In fact, it is worthy to strive for victory

Let's be great with open budget

Happy holidays to Open Budget.

Sleep, laziness, is alien to us

At night he struck, Kalvak hides

It was a support, a pillar, father and mother

Happy holiday to the people of Kalvak.

My elders, in prayer

Praise be to the Creator

Hold your chest high, let it touch on Shabbat

Happy holiday to Haji Baqijan.

Dear Russia, my kind country

Three thousand brothers in your arms

Ten million in kindness

Happy holiday, brothers and sisters abroad.

There were those who stood and laughed

He died from the blow of victory

The enemy withered without throwing his spear

Happy holidays to you, dear friends.

Come on, sister, tell me the number

Hey dad, hey bro, back to the gift

Say six digits, SMS

Happy holiday to a familiar stranger.

Chustu, Kosonsoi, Fairy Garden

It even climbed, Tian~ Shan Mountain

He went as needed, Ocean River

Happy holiday to my Jafokash people.

Shuhratjon, Shavkatjon, my dear liver

At the most difficult time, thank you, dear

My sad heart felt compassion

Dear friends, happy holiday.

And many more, guys

I agree with the initiative

Someone worked great, someone a little less

Those who did not write names, happy holiday.

19 thousand milestones, the moment of victory

The conscience of every Khojad

Celebrate today, honor

Congratulations on your victory, dear fellow countryman.

(May 7 ~ went down in history as the day of solidarity of Khojand Mfy people.)

MY SECURITY.

The cousin opened the sleeping bride

A beautiful flower rose from the ground.

It's a swinging swing

I'm sorry, I'm sorry, I'm sorry.

A cold person can't be bothered

The last blind will not melt in the dirty hill.

I don't have a mind to stop it

My hair is a bit of a hurry.

Open your delicate autumn

A red scarf and a beautiful shirt.

Don't rush, don't bow your head

My hair is a bit of a hurry.

This dune has a lot of dusty properties

There is a lot of dust and knife-wielding muscles in front of you.

There are many passes that cost the flower frame

My hair is a bit of a hurry.

MUHAMMAD YUSUF, WHO DID NOT STOP CREATION.

Celebrities live like fire

Takes a step forward

It starts with faith, creativity, and intelligence

Not satisfied with life, Muhammad Yusuf

Muhammad Yusuf, who did not stop creating.

My friend, you had the right to live a long time

May God bless you

Creativity and attention

Muhammad Yusuf, who did not write the poem.

I saw Zebo in your poems

In front of me, I saw a ghost in my dream

I saw that Layla I was looking for

Muhammad Yusuf, who was looking for deals.

You taught me to love peace

You rocked the tulip

You've lost your sense of humor

Muhammad Yusuf, familiar with love.

I am a noble, dignified, noble school

Rustam, a poet in poetry

In a word, I am handsome

Muhammad who drew the human figure.

You have taken a deep place in the hearts of the people

How many poems you could not say

You have made the poor knots sad

He didn't put the pen down

Muhammad Yusuf.

Muhammad Yusuf is not satisfied with life.

Muhammad Yusuf, the favorite poet of the Uzbek people dedicated to the 69th anniversary of his birth.

HONOR YOUR MOTHER.

For mother's hymn, I have many songs

The street where mother walked, kiss the soil

Mother's every word, every request

Respect your mother, mother is great.

Mother is the basis of the world

A baby's cry, a mother's word

When you are a bride, hello mom

Respect your mother, mother is great.

Honor the mother, the mother is great

Born from mother, human being after all

The divine three letters, the breed named "mother".

Respect your mother, mother is great.

You were a piece of meat, you baby jussa

You grew up without a father, sad and sad.

You will be alone, even if your mother passes

Mothers are a treasure, a mother is great.

Today your mother is alive, take her blessing

Always listen to Pandu's advice

You are beautiful, let your tongue be good

Mothers are a treasure, a mother is great.

Don't say hello to your mother

There is intelligence ~ foresight, this is in a healthy body

The house is a dungeon, don't be on the street

Mothers are a treasure, a mother is a noble.

WAR has begun.

41 years. It's morning.

Chain gate, combs are not good.

What happened, let's find out who it is

The war has started, disaster to the country

Hitler beetle mustache, that casofat.

Eru~ in a blue suit, arrows viz-viz

The battle was joined at noon yesterday

Former USSR, world star

The war has started, disaster to the country

Enjoy life, don't be ignorant.

The white man lit the fire of war

What a hideous creature he is

Tailless, scabby, and the end is horrible.

The war has started, disaster to the country

Five years of the world, a wasted disaster.

20: Million Martyr Cemetery

The land is old silence, winter, prison

For happy bloods, this day is flowery.

A disaster has begun for the country

Let the name fly, the name of war.

Uzbek boy in terrible battles

He was not afraid of the enemy, his breast shield

Uzbek has justified the great name and the blood

The war has started, disaster to the country

Protection of the country, habit to the east.

HUSBAND~WIFE, DOUBLE WING ..

(Dedicated to International Family Day.)

Men know that the cat is harmless

Sometimes he looks like a wild lion.

The husband is unhappy, and the woman is rude

After all, he is a young man, an intelligent person.

Wife.

Your father is coming, come, father

If your stomach is hungry, I will swim pilaf.

Peace be upon you, a prayer in the heart

In a sweet smile,

my words are one.

Good news, our daughter Barna

He got a grade "5" in mathematics.

Hold your hand, my eldest Rana

Oliygokh. A student. Secluded from the village.

Male.

Thanks bro, I'm fine

Thank God I found you.

I love you, patient and understanding

You don't blame me, you don't look for me.

You know, for now, I have a need

Our new garden, my mud house.

My two daughters and I are partners together

We'll get it later, livelihood item.

My daughters are smart, you understand

Just hold on, support by my side

Alright friends, I'm dressed

I need a replacement for my family's happiness.

Author.

You have the bridle of the wild lion

Put your feminine art to work right away.

Be flirtatious and smile

After all, you are a hunter, let your husband hunt.

R O' M O L IS OKAY.

Shabnam, the scarf suits you well

They look at the past with longing.

They cheat when you walk without a headscarf

It's true, the scarf suits you.

A white scarf makes you look beautiful

In a hurry, the flowers are blooming

"Moon" is running away from me because he has a beautiful girl

Shabnam, the scarf suits you well.

Your hair will also rest in the scarf

Dream, hope, good will, brings to mind

The propagandist leaves all the girls behind

Shabnam, the scarf suits you well.

You wear a hijab with a chin, wrap a scarf

If you don't believe it, please ask

The stone is reflected in the mirror, Shabnam is excellent~ a

Shabnam, the scarf suits you well.

Your mother honors you, from the evil eye

Shield your pure name from bad words

They fight for your honor, from a bad face

Shabnam, the scarf suits you well.

If you respect me as a teacher

If you know that I am starting on the right path

If you wear a scarf and walk with ibo

Shabnam, the scarf suits you well.

A student ran away.

A student ran away

He spilled his bag

He went over the gate

You need to know why

It is necessary to take concrete measures.

Or was he upset with the teacher

Do not burn excess laundry

Horse hooves, takamidi

Why did you skip class, comrade?

Not to mention, the situation is dire.

Did he fight with his friend?

Did the girls laugh at him

Did they know anything wrong?

You need to find a reader

It is necessary to close the chest.

Poor, crooked mouth

If he finds a shirt, his shirt is torn

However, his face is pale

He was always silent

He was living in a house

Maybe it's at home

The virgin mother is thinking

Tomorrow is the day

The family needs help

The reader needs sympathy.

There are many such students

Don't stand on the sidelines

Don't gossip too much

Now we need to find a solution

Need, need, need again.

A stingy person.

A stingy person does not put up with stinginess.

He does not fear the consequences of a good deed.

Invisibility does not stop evil

Be careful among us, miser.

Unintentionally, a bad step.

A small scorpion that is always ready to attack

The poison is obvious to any friend in the queue

Be careful, you are a target

Be careful, stingy among us.

The color is golden, it greets the shade

He will see the guilty in you

He is ready to know and not know

Be careful, stingy among us.

High-flying praise today

Enjoy a lavish party for free

Slow down with one minor mistake

Be careful, stingy among us.

There is a narration, it doesn't hurt

garden

It's a stain on the heart that won't improve or change

Not even a school, but a life lesson

Be careful, stingy among us

Unintentionally, a bad step.

Road trip.

I am the earth, if you know

Give me mercy if you know the cure.

You will be fine without me

You rub dirt on my face.

I am the biggest road in Khojand

I carved a deep muddy lake.

I'm bad quality, I'm ugly, that's it

My heart is broken oh oh oh.

Drivers are nervous

It is impossible, he can barely walk.

Kindergarten child fell down see

Do not find a straight path.

Ikram is my pink panoch

Tell me what's wrong with me.

After all, you are also a child of Khujand

A favorite of the neighborhood.

As long as you are there, I am sure

My helper, my joy.

It will be a beautiful road, of course

Ghurbat will be forgotten.

Years pass, dreams are many

When you order, the guys are ready.

A different love for my repair

Is there a check, the promise is over.

I like the neighboring roads

Namanganlik is like a prospect

Be a black asphalt road.

I look forward to you.

Hojandi's young girls

We were waiting for such moments.

Early in the morning, when the waters sprinkle

If the cars pass straight.

Walk out of my neighborhood, out of my way

Donate at weddings.

No offense to Orzu, I will wait again

I will write poems for you again.

Ikromjon, chairman of Khojand MFI

Longings of the main road of Kolkhovuz neighborhood to Isokov.

Tray bearer.

He doesn't have a clear idea, he doesn't care

A cautious person is a fearful person

It's like varnish mixed with house paint

In a prosperous world

On the stage of life, in a live movie.

It looks like a man, the shape is like a candle

Always inclined to compromise

"AKA" I admire your work

In a prosperous world

In the movie that plays on the stage of life.

Dumin likillatar, an example is a fox

When it doesn't work, it's funny

This is the white foam on the surface of the water

Lagandardar lives in the world

In the movie that plays on the stage of life.

He praises the chief and lifts him up

The official sits close to the leader

He sprinkles saliva and swallows faith

In a prosperous world

In the movie that plays on the stage of life.

Tepakal, grinning, I'm your dog

I will follow you, go myself

I won't bite you yet, I'm your lice.

Lagandardar, live in the world

In the movie that plays on the stage of life.

Uneducated, uneducated omi

In any case, it is dry, the roof is higher

Three or four soums of charity is paid at least

In a prosperous, living world

In the movie that plays on the stage of life.

QO'LIGULUSTA.

Otabek is a skilled florist

Iron body, patients, turn one hundred.

Finds a remedy for a broken car

Ready. Ready to go, hood closes.

Uncle, the role of the car is broken

The transmitter cable is disconnected.

The black lacettini contact is faulty

Right now, it will take ten minutes to recover.

White Damascus, radiator hole

In the old Moskvich, a non-closing door.

The gas distributor needs to be renewed

Tired battery, need charging.

You have a gas pump that is working poorly

The driver shakes his head miserably.

The valve is stuck, needs to be fixed

My apprentice brothers, help with the repair.

Zhiguli's car hit a rock

The main frame is shifted to the left.

His lamp burned out, the blue Damasni

Ready to go, drive Kamaz.

This happens every day

Every car needs treatment.

Humble, equal to everyone, very cute

He lives in the bosom of his father and mother.

MOTHER HUSBAND.

Why are you nervous, shaking, husband

We need you, my dear, husband

Sinful servants say, "Keep it yourself."

What are you worried about, you shake, husband.

Just yesterday there was an earthquake in Turku

Countless people, buried, died

The face of the people of the Black Sea has faded.

Why are you restless, shaking?

husband

Have we found your golden soil?

Didn't we tear your treasure and close it?

Haven't we found a solution to peace?

Why are you restless, shaking?

husband

After all, you are a mother, you have a warm heart

Your people will live in repentance

Forgive us, you have mercy in the palm of your hand

Why are you restless, shaking?

husband

Please, mother earth, don't shake anymore

My eyeball is a treasure, don't cry anymore

Accept our prayer, don't hide anymore

Don't worry, don't shake, husband.

Open budget.

(Regarding Nurilo Nuri's poem "Vote")

An unexpected game was released

Everyone seemed to be gambling.

He gathered the team

Open budget, open budget.

Zir runs everywhere

We don't have time to comb our hair

Baby does not cry to look

Open budget, open budget.

Let there be a thousand voices

Ten to you, ten to him

Duration is only one day

Open budget, open budget.

Open the door, brother, who are you?

No one, why are you quiet?

Runs day and night

Open budget, open budget.

Brother came out frowning

What is needed?

Did it start, collected again

Open budget, open budget.

He started talking embarrassedly

He stuttered and nodded

Text message

Open budget, open budget.

Olapar also chased

He chased down the narrow street

The country is over

Open budget, open budget.

The plan worked out amazingly

I don't intend to be impartial

Sokmas is no longer boss

Open budget, open budget.

SUMALAK.

Sumac in Doshkazon

There are seven qualifications around

Spring has come to me

He died before he could.

Forty stones in sumac

An eyebrow that puts the moon to shame

Dosh around the pot

The donation was distributed.

Those who ate, those who did not

They didn't leave even at night

Magic wand in hand

Those who are not satisfied.

The flame in the hearth

Lapar says new

Seven and a half is a whole

Sumalak sanga manga.

Sumalak vaqur~ vaqur

It's cooked, call everyone

Hey neighborhood, neighbor

Try it, of course it's hot.

QUEEN OF T U N .

I am a driver every day

A passenger girl raised her hand.

That day it was dark

I don't know now, there is a trace in my heart.

Two children are two descendants

He knew the key to happiness in education.

He blew it, that's it

Fortunately, fate smiled.

A single woman is lonely

His patience is broken in tests.

Her name is Rana, maybe she is Nargiz

Like a solid stone, it did not break.

A broken dream from that day

I think of him involuntarily.

If I can help, she's a badass

I am thinking of the house where the woman fell.

Why now the queen of the night

They met in the night, not the day.

Maybe it's true, maybe it's a trick

Honestly, my heart is in it.

If you need my name, Tahir

When will it reach Venus?

It is revealed to meet from absent

When will the heart agree.

TO'Y.

Murgak Nihal opened his eyes to the sky

My strong maple, we send you a wish

You are my double wing, we need you

Happy two-year wedding anniversary.

Different test, endurance score

If you grow, you will bloom

An example of the shining sun

Happy two-year wedding anniversary.

A short time, how much is a fan

How many stars are there, so are your wings

You are opening, my rose, an open flower bud.

Happy two-year wedding anniversary.

Greetings to my mother, my flower is one piece

Our hearts are full of happy fans

Mother Musharraf is in the center of the stage

Happy two-year wedding anniversary.

An example of Za Nurliy, Jumagul aya

I don't care if I have a chance to talk

Be in the language of Zahirnafas

Happy two-year wedding anniversary.

I think about Gulnara

I'm looking for love poems

I will play laparga with him

Happy two-year wedding anniversary.

Bibirajab Elbekova is proud determination

The poems he wrote are intense

An oriental custom for an Uzbek woman

Happy two-year wedding anniversary.

An innocent woman named Adalat

I looked at it three or four times

Tell me what I think

Happy two-year wedding anniversary.

Love from Ahadova Samar and sugar

The paper is in wood, the pen is made of sugar

The heart notes are from the four-bar

Happy two-year wedding anniversary.

Muhayyo Begalieva, there is a reflection of the sun

A loving heart has a picture of love

Mushoira, every day he has a problem

Happy two-year wedding anniversary.

A strange sound from Karakalpak

Burns, burns, Hayotbakhsh Barno

The song of friendship is good

Happy two-year wedding anniversary

A beautiful landscape in a green forest

The singing of a ball of birds is delicious

Nodirabonu's navo is soz~a

Happy two-year wedding anniversary.

A star means a full moon

The beauty revealed in poetry

Tell me a beautiful poem

Happy two-year wedding anniversary.

Watching on the sidelines, Mahmudjan is a teacher

Applause, inspiring songs

How much I can write about this person

Happy two-year wedding anniversary.

Guli Nigor, Latofat, Dildora Rahman

They are princesses, their owners are khans

I am surprised to know more closely

Happy two-year wedding anniversary.

Shoyadbek, Zakirjon, ibn Asadullah

Good luck, Koshkhanot

the witness

May Allah protect the creative people

Happy two-year wedding anniversary

Over two hundred, Kosh's wing

Friendship bonds, goal habit

Two friends ride this horse in the saddle

Happy two-year wedding anniversary.

We don't know how many hearts there are

How many wishes are new poems

We are one whole as long as the wrists

Happy two-year wedding anniversary.

Like Juma Aripov, a professional friend

A trusted confidant in good times and bad

A maple root, a leaf is blood

Happy two-year wedding anniversary.

He is still young and has the fierceness of a lion in his heart

Willful Eldar have the power of the land

He has a great country like his mother

Happy two-year wedding anniversary.

O' T T I Z U Ch T A. (33 items)

(A funnier poem.)

To thirty-three women

We caught an elegant red flower.

Not a flower, but a flower

We waited for a woman's love.

Beauty in every way

There is a symbol of love.

Bright pink face

The owner has a mirror.

March 8 is the day

It is not necessary to pass the class.

Go home, rest

The leader says nothing.

Today is the spring holiday

Hello.

With courtesy, respect

Greetings to you.

(Dear and respectable women of school 4, you are sincerely congratulated by professional teachers.)

MY SCIENTIST, MY DEAR ZULFIYA.

(Loyalty singer) competition.

He shouts, breaking the silence

Sometimes by car, sometimes by walking

Foresaw the future

My scholar, my dear Zulfiya.

Two writers, two great people

What a disaster in Olimjon

Two horses worthy of recognition

My scholar and writer Zulfiyam.

Happiness and luck are the singer of joy

A look at the world, a singer of pleasure

He is a singer of excitement towards a lively creation

My scholar Hamid, my happy Zulfiya.

When the apricot blossoms, sweet gooseberry

Finish your poems until spring

The queen of the word, beautiful muncha

My beautiful Zulfiyam, the harbinger of spring.

May this land bloom and live

One is Aigul, the other is Bakhtiyar

There is a rule to say such a couple

Zulfiyam, who loved the poet Olimjon.

O' X Sh A Y D I.

My double wing, on a swallow's wing

Horseman's, woolly straw

on his horse

I miss you, dear human race

It seems that spring and happiness have arrived.

The high mountains are proud

It's a strange pride these days.

I don't understand, maybe that's happiness.

It seems that spring and happiness have arrived.

Mother calls the sun of the earth

Pulls a sleeping ladybug

Pure hearts delight.

It seems that spring and happiness have arrived.

The world is getting brighter day by day

Farmers plant crops

A lover can make his heart melt

It seems that spring and happiness have arrived.

THREE KILO, SEVEN HUNDRED GRAMS

Three kilos, about four kilos

The rhizome is the largest head of the grape.

Exactly three kilos, seven hundred grams

I created in my garden, the stone of tamal

The buyer's brothers are holding each other by the collar

It is suitable for viticulture news.

"Give it to me," he said

Do a favor to the Uzbek farmer.

I am a farmer of Khojand land

Learning the art and science of farming.

I like to work.

A particle of my people, a spark is burning.

I picked grape varieties

The book of life, scientifically followed.

I didn't know if it was Sarah's product

Think and correct the mistake you made.

Beautiful red in the heat of July

Ishkam queen, as if a bride.

Be careful, baby on the lips

In the morning dew, a silver bead.

One grain does not fit in your mouth

Your tongue will stick, from the taste buds.

I planted it in the yard, a vine

The sun is not visible, through the garden.

Thank God, he is healthy

I am still in the lap of work.

What I said is not praise, not praise

I will throw it in the joy of my heart.

I Ch U V Ch I.

I drink every day

Both lying and sitting.

It doesn't matter whether it's day or night

Sometimes I drink full.

When my friend pours

I will not return his hand.

When the day comes

Find a way.

I drink all day long

I don't overspend.

No matter how much I drink

I don't like it at all.

Don't say I drank like that

The end will be woe.

If you know, this is what I drank

There will be ninety-five teas.

Ch E K U V Ch I.

Asking smokers

Alivoy doesn't like it.

Ask him to smoke

Can't do it, Solivoy.

Immediately give a cigarette

Zazhigal says where.

Once your check arrives

He says call me.

Let's have fun

Dawn called in the morning.

Let's drink at least

Soli shouted.

Ask for a cigarette

You made me live

What, I'll give it

My lips to smoke.

I FOUND IT

I found a date, walking through the fields

The door of my heart's love, knock on it and sort it.

Don't jump on the stone now, don't get tired, my dear.

A delicate sprout of cypress,

I'm a fish from the flower.

I planted basil in my yard for you

I am sorry for the sufferings, you will not be able to breastfeed.

Break the chains of grief, let's fly to the moon together.

Let's embrace the palace of happiness, which does not give us a handle in the dream.

White dress, tender heart, fly swan.

I am waiting like an eagle, my castle is comfortable at the top.

The flight of the eagle and the swan,

a new legend in the east,

It's nice to have a swan

I'm a prisoner, mastona.

Happy Eid Mubarak.

We are in the Prophet's youth

We are near the cemetery

Our fellow Muslim

Happy Eid Mubarak.

The custom of praying five times a day

Pleasure is in heaven

The bliss of two hearts

Happy Eid Mubarak.

On the occasion of two holidays

During Hajj

Death is in the coffin

Happy Eid Mubarak.

A living soul to be slaughtered

Blood in God's way

Being happy

Happy Eid Mubarak.

God knows our way

Our hands are in prayer

Our tongue rejoices

Happy Eid Mubarak.

Don't be sad my friend

Don't die prematurely

Do not be ashamed of honor

Happy Eid Mubarak.

It is great to go to the Kaaba

good luck to us

our face is bright as the moon

Happy Eid Mubarak.

Let's live in peace

Let's bow down

Let's make a donation

Happy Eid Mubarak.

Remember the past

Make the poor happy

Bless this day

Happy Eid Mubarak.

My dear co-religionists, believing Muslims. May you have a blessed "KURBON" Eid holiday, my God, stay healthy.

I LOVE YOU ANYWAY.

I love you anyway

Even if you are superior to me

I will walk with you in your imagination

My scriptures, even if you don't read them.

I love you anyway

Remember the day you met for the first time.

I put my hand in your hand

Wait for me again at the Youth Center.

I love you one by one

As Navoi loved Guli

Look in my heart, I can feel it

Don't push me away, don't push me away.

Anyway, I love you

You are the most beautiful person in the world.

I will look at your portrait

A distant star, like yourself.

I love you anyway

Put on a flower horn, it's fine

I look at the sky and see your beauty

He looked at you with desire.

I love you anyway

I want to write only about you.

No matter how far away, I will come

I want to touch your lips

OFFICERS OF INTERIOR AFFAIRS.

An authoritative office, order is embodied

New benefits, to name a few

If my work is done well and I come back happy

Thank you, internal affairs officers.

Shoyadbek, Nargiza, Babur, Daniyor

I wish you good luck in your noble profession

Don't take off your lucky belt

Good luck, internal affairs officers.

Your honest cocktail deserves praise

Handsome, handsome, beautiful uniform

Adequate monthly, set by the state

Kudos to you, internal affairs officers.

Don't take your nerve from the client

Be open-faced, don't be arrogant

Don't take the inevitable to heart

Thank you, internal affairs officers.

Our roads are smooth, our moods are high

First of all, we ourselves, our car is healthy

Do not stay in the heart, pain, dust, stain

Good luck, internal affairs officers.

You, my people, are my daily balm

Legal documents, be strong

Don't get tired, don't be tired, don't be tired.

Kudos to you, internal affairs officers.

Kazakh beauty.

It is different to look at the Kazakh beauty

Combing Sunbul's hair is different

It's different if it suits my pain

Where are you from, Kazakh beauty?

"Oh my dear"

I'm wearing a flowery vest

If I don't find it today, I'm helpless, I'm humiliated

Where are you from, Kazakh beauty?

A skilled rider on Armugon

Loosen the reins, ride the horse

The date of the Kazakh is perfect for me

Where are you from, Kazakh beauty?

Biya's flowers are a cure for my skin

Green nature, calmness to pain

Thirsty, dombira, melodious navo

Where are you from, Kazakh beauty?

Parivash my beauty, happiness is in our hands

If you agree, a deal is on its way

Let's live double wings, in our yard

Where are you from, Kazakh beauty?

HEART OF STONE

No matter how big you are, don't be arrogant

Anyway, I know you think of me.

Do not divide my words, my poem

Your mind is on the phone, like me.

It depends on your height and your mind

I am writing poems, you know.

Don't hide your ugly face yet

Out of anger, you are beating.

I wish you had a pistol in your hand

Torture of suffering, you are in pain.

How many did you try to shoot?

You make me drunk with my love.

You can't kill, man

Put the gun barrel to my forehead.

I am a prisoner of your love, my body is a target

"I can't live without you" think in your heart.

Your hands were shaking and you reacted

One step behind me, bottomless winter.

Goodbye, my love, you hugged me

Red from crying, our way is free.

AWESOME, CARDIOLOGIST.

It is the taste of the heart

Do you need a voice?

Cardiologist clean

Well done Ulugbek.

A master of his craft

One hundred at reception

Heart, heart angel

I went to Ulugbek at five.

I didn't know the others

I have not seen such a doctor

I did not wait in line

Thank you Ulugbek.

Years of experience

New, new result

Nurse Samida

Well done Ulugbek.

Knowledgeable in medicine

Teacher Hakmi Luqman

This moment is a balm to the heart

I went to Ulugbek at five.

The nerve fiber is severed

Blood circulation is disturbed

Man is made of blood

Thanks to Ulugbek.

Mr. Chief Medical Officer

I have one request

You are the only one in the meeting

Well done Ulugbek.

This poem is dedicated to Ulugbek Ahadov, a skilled cardiologist.

UZBEK OTHELLO or HANDKERCHIEF

To Desdemona.

Am I black, I will choke

Stupid, find the handkerchief and look.

In a dirty bed, I feel ashamed

You made a white handkerchief, black.

He knew, feed him

Now I'm black, you're a handkerchief.

Nozu~ karashmeli, frown

I loved you, how much and how much.

Yago.

You entered my wife's bosom, shamelessly

You betrayed your dear friend.

Two friends do not swear

After all, good luck with my love.

Now it's either death or right

I gave you, Desdemona.

Ok I'm leaving, ok I'm unfair

Oh, how much is this handkerchief?

Tursunali says, save your love

Don't leave the world to YaGOs.

Uzbek Othello, save love

Don't take away the clean handkerchief.

NURSE GIRL.

Nurse girl Zilola

Very agile, cute.

I'll take it, a bunch of tulips

An example in the sky is the moon.

Just look at it

In front of women.

How much applause

The sick father is in the head.

It measures blood pressure

Tonometer shafts.

Well, if it is normal.

Lively girl thoughts.

Syringe u,, drugs

He injects slowly.

Necessary medicine black

There will be a medicine.

Medical nurse

Heart pain.

Family blonde

Angel of the owner.

(The poem is dedicated to Zilola Naqibova, nurse of the regional cardiology center)

LATER REGRET.

I know my fault, I left

I was infamous for a second

My first love, shoot me.

For the honor of masculinity, I brought the isnad.

My student days, beautiful evenings.

Tired of reading, unnecessary sorrows.

Red from the heat, the city air

Dilbar malagim love trade.

What a fool I am

Worth a penny, disgusting class.

To the god of love, I have committed treason

I think about them all the time.

I was a rabbit heart, I was scared

Being brave, I did not reveal this secret

Because I was engaged to a village girl

How I looked at his face.

I admire your strong will

Shame on my goal, lifeless expression.

You left without saying a word

Where have you been all these years?

That village girl is unfaithful

He ruined my sweet life

A year later, my life turned upside down

As long as there is someone talking, I am left for the isnad.

I read the news in the newspaper yesterday

You are the head of a large company

Now I'm sad, poor, poor

I was fired from my job, I received a bribe.

"Dad," said someone behind me

someone

Just in case, I looked right away

I have my son and you in front of me

It's like in my dream.

CARDIO CENTER.

It's a great time

Palace. Crystal coshana

My eyes are burning

Thanks to the cardio center.

In the chapter on perfection

In the medical wing

In the book of honesty

A thousand thanks to Akmaljon.

I have been to this place

I saw the treatment

I asked the patient

Thanks to the management.

Practice guards

Hippocratic caravans

Heroes of the day

Many thanks to the doctors.

If it's bad, it's in the body

Health in every body

No pain, right now

Thanks to the nurses.

A perfect angel in Oza

The gaze is on every corner

Middle-class in everything

Many thanks to the staff.

Don't get sick first

Please bow

God heals and heals

Thanks to Cardiocenter.

He built a hospital

Allah has shown confidence

He made Namangan laugh

Many thanks to Solikhan.

(Namangan Region Cardiology Center R. E. Kh
I bow to the doctors of the department and to Akmaljon personally.)

I HAVE A MIND

This world itself is beautiful

It is more beautiful to live

The word "I love" is beautiful

I have a heart for Shahnoza.

Malak was born by the moon

Maybe the makeup is infected

Have you ever dreamed of being beautiful?

I have a heart for Shahnoza.

At a glance, the heart is broken

Jamali is speechless

There is a trace on his finger

I have a heart for Shahnoza.

The lesson of marriage

Red cheeks

Beauty is a companion

I have a heart for Shahnoza.

I can't wait

I hold bouquets

I can read poetry and ghazals

I have a heart for Shahnoza.

Dreams are one world

She is a princess, I am a khan

We will be happy every moment

I have a heart for Shahnoza.

Black eyebrows bow, bow

I'm looking for it

Shahnoz is good, I am bad

I have a heart for Shahnoza.

A sweet word in the language

Alhamdulillah greetings

Cooking girl food

I have a heart for Shahnoza.

Hijab scarf on the head

Shy, reserved

Dwarf condition on right face

I have a heart for Shahnoza.

I'll wait on the side of the road

In the wedding ring wedding

He is high, I am below

I have a heart for Shahnoza.

He gave us both happiness

He gave the throne in addition to happiness

He made a covenant with faith

I have a heart for Shahnoza.

ASILABONU.

The intelligence of a doctor

Understanding with deep thought

Human virtue, saifu~ generosity

Cardiologist doctor, Asilabonu.

A great place, great concern

Goodness to man, daily work

Two polaponi, a love bird

Cardiologist doctor, Asilabonu.

As a woman, my mind raced

My blood pressure suddenly increased

In the river of love, the wave overflowed.

Cardiologist doctor, Asilabonu.

Servant of Allah, Islamic verse

Faith is in faith, happiness is.

Kalimai Shahodat, a daily habit

Cardiologist doctor, Asilabonu.

Hear me say this word out loud

A beautiful family, order incarnate

Honor the woman, the noble one

Cardiologist doctor, Asilabonu.

Chief doctor, I have one request for you

Say at the meeting, I owe you a thank you

I am sick, I have a verse for you

Cardiologist doctor, Asilabonu.

WEDDINGS, ENDING WOES.

Hey dad, have you come?

Wait~ wait, I have four eyes.

Today I wrote expenses for a big wedding

Take care of yourself.

Tepa, in the neighborhood, Oybodok is fat

Chiranma Oysanam, our beta said.

I have a dream, you will see

You know Satang Oysanam at the wedding.

Millions on the list, heads turned

Yes, you are a fool, your language is rich.

You see, I borrowed money from four of my neighbors

Don't open my eyes, the debts are off my neck.

Let the money go, don't let the reputation go

Let the father and the husband swallow what he said

Our grain goes to seven neighborhoods

Borrow more, then that's enough.

There was a wedding, the table, everything is fine

Well-known artists, at your service

table.

Special dishes, even from Paris.

Anko clan also came from abroad.

The wedding didn't go by without a fuss

There was a knock on the door.

Half a billion expenses, what to do now

Bring the rope, die without warning.

Don't spoil the goose

If there is a measure, a calculation, weddings will take place.

To the house of debts, the wedding held

It's such a pity, it's a pity.

(In some cases, such incidents occur in families due to the fault of women.)

G'ANIM

I have many enemies, I know for sure

It is flying in my head like a raven.

Laughing at the tip of the tongue, smiling, familiar

He is waiting for me to fade away.

I didn't know if it was a man or a woman

It is now ready to be crushed.

He is a tyrant and a tyrant

In the Bay of Sorrow, the horse runs.

If I hold the magic mirror, Bashara

From the serum of pain, a broken ocean.

Lice, mites, aphids live in whey

Do not expect good from him.

A black snake bites

Laugh in poison, dagger in your back

If it dies, it will bite.

Stab your chest with all your might.

Allegedly dear, blunt nonsense

The heart is darkened by hatred.

He pulls an ax in spite of your face

He is determined to destroy you.

Death of the eagle, feast for the dogs

He lives in Uzbek, that's the story.

Don't be surprised by the content of the poem

It's a real human book, maybe you should read it.

www.ingramcontent.com/pod-product-compliance
Lightning Source LLC
LaVergne TN
LVHW010214070526
838199LV00062B/4585